Junior Drug Awareness
HOW TO SAY NO

Junior Drug Awareness

Alcohol

Amphetamines and Other Uppers

Crack and Cocaine

Ecstasy and Other Designer Drugs

Heroin

How to Get Help

How to Say No

Inhalants and Solvents

LSD, PCP, and Other Hallucinogens

Marijuana

Nicotine and Cigarettes

Pain Relievers, Diet Pills, and
    Other Over-the-Counter Drugs

Prozac and Other Antidepressants

Steroids

Valium and Other Downers

Junior Drug Awareness

HOW TO SAY NO

Introduction by **BARRY R. McCAFFREY**
Director, Office of National Drug Control Policy

Foreword by **STEVEN L. JAFFE, M.D.**
Senior Consulting Editor,
Professor of Child and Adolescent Psychiatry, Emory University

Virginia Aronson

Chelsea House Publishers
Philadelphia

CHELSEA HOUSE PUBLISHERS
Editor in Chief Stephen Reginald
Production Manager Pamela Loos
Director of Photography Judy L. Hasday
Art Director Sara Davis
Managing Editor James D. Gallagher
Senior Production Editor LeeAnne Gelletly

Staff for HOW TO SAY NO
Senior Editor Therese De Angelis
Associate Art Director Takeshi Takahashi
Designer Keith Trego
Picture Researcher Patricia Burns
Cover Designer Keith Trego

Cover photo © 1997 R.B. Studio/The Stock Market

The Chelsea House World Wide Web site address is
http://www.chelseahouse.com

First Printing
1 3 5 7 9 8 6 4 2

Library of Congress Cataloging-in-Publication Data
Aronson, Virginia.
How to say no / Virginia Aronson.
80 pp.   cm. — (Junior drug awareness)
Includes bibliographical references and index.
Summary: Charts, graphs, statistics, and text describe
current drug use and abuse, explain the dangers and
damaging effects of illegal drugs, tobacco products, and
alcohol, and suggest ways to avoid them.
ISBN 0-7910-5202-8
1. Drug abuse—United States—Juvenile literature.
2. Drug abuse—United States—Prevention—Juvenile
literature. [1. Drug abuse. 2. Alcoholism.] I. Title.
II. Series.
HV5809.5.A76 1999
362.29'083'50973—dc21   98-50452
                                                CIP
                                                AC

CONTENTS

by Barry R. McCaffrey
Director, Office of National
Drug Control Policy

STAYING AWAY FROM ILLEGAL DRUGS, TOBACCO PRODUCTS, AND ALCOHOL

Good health allows you to be as strong, happy, smart, and skillful as you can possibly be. The worst thing about illegal drugs is that they damage people from the inside. Our bodies and minds are wonderful, complicated systems that run like finely tuned machines when we take care of ourselves.

Doctors prescribe legal drugs, called medicines, to heal us when we become sick, but dangerous chemicals that are not recommended by doctors, nurses, or pharmacists are called illegal drugs. These drugs cannot be bought in stores because they harm different organs of the body, causing illness or even death. Illegal drugs, such as marijuana, cocaine or "crack," heroin, methamphetamine ("meth"), and other dangerous substances are against the law because they affect our ability to think, work, play, sleep, or eat.

If anyone ever offers you illegal drugs or any kind of pills, liquids, substances to smoke, or shots to inject into your body, tell them you're not interested. You should report drug pushers—people who distribute these poisons—to parents, teachers, police, coaches, clergy, or other adults whom you trust.

Cigarettes and alcohol are also illegal for youngsters. Tobacco products and drinks like wine, beer, and liquor are particularly harmful for children and teenagers because their bodies, especially their nervous systems, are still developing. For this reason, young people are more likely to be hurt by illicit drugs—including cigarettes and alcohol. These two products kill more people—from cancer, and automobile accidents caused by intoxicated drivers—than all other drugs combined. We say about drug use: "Users are losers." Be a winner and stay away from illegal drugs, tobacco products, and alcoholic beverages.

Here are four reasons why you shouldn't use illegal drugs:

- Illegal drugs can cause brain damage.
- Illegal drugs are "psychoactive." This means that they change your personality or the way you feel. They also impair your judgment. While under the influence of drugs, you are more likely to endanger your life or someone else's. You will also be less able to protect yourself from danger.
- Many illegal drugs are addictive, which means that once a person starts taking them, stopping is extremely difficult. An addict's body craves the drug and becomes dependent upon it. The illegal drug–user may become sick if the drug is discontinued and so may become a slave to drugs.

- Some drugs, called "gateway" substances, can lead a person to take more-dangerous drugs. For example, a 12-year-old who smokes marijuana is 79 times more likely to have an addiction problem later in life than a child who never tries marijuana.

Here are some reasons why you shouldn't drink alcoholic beverages, including beer and wine coolers:

- Alcohol is the second leading cause of death in our country. More than 100,000 people die every year because of drinking.
- Adolescents are twice as likely as adults to be involved in fatal alcohol-related car crashes.
- Half of all assaults against girls or women involve alcohol.
- Drinking is illegal if you are under the age of 21. You could be arrested for this crime.

Here are three reasons why you shouldn't smoke cigarettes:

- Nicotine is highly addictive. Once you start smoking, it is very hard to stop, and smoking cigarettes causes lung cancer and other diseases. Tobacco- and nicotine-related diseases kill more than 400,000 people every year.
- Each day, 3,000 kids begin smoking. One-third of these youngsters will probably have their lives shortened because of tobacco use.
- Children who smoke cigarettes are almost six times more likely to use other illegal drugs than kids who don't smoke.

If your parents haven't told you how they feel about the dangers of illegal drugs, ask them. One of every 10 kids aged 12 to 17 is using illegal drugs. They do not understand the risks they are taking with their health and their lives. However, the vast majority of young people in America are smart enough to figure out that drugs, cigarettes, and alcohol could rob them of their future. Be your body's best friend: guard your mental and physical health by staying away from drugs.

WHY SHOULD I LEARN ABOUT DRUGS?

Steven L. Jaffe, M.D., Senior Consulting Editor,
Professor of Child and Adolescent Psychiatry,
Emory University

Your grandparents and great-grandparents did not think much about "drug awareness." That's because drugs, to most of them, simply meant "medicine."

Of the three types of drugs, medicine is the good type. Medicines such as penicillin and aspirin promote healing and help sick people get better.

Another type of drug is obviously bad for you because it is poison. Then there are the kinds of drugs that fool you, such as marijuana and LSD. They make you feel good, but they harm your body and brain.

Our great crisis today is that this third category of drugs has become widely abused. Drugs of abuse are everywhere, not just in rough neighborhoods. Many teens are introduced to drugs by older brothers, sisters, friends, or even friends' parents. Some people may use only a little bit of a drug, but others who inherited a tendency to become addicted may move on to using drugs all the time. If a family member is or was an alcoholic or an addict, a young person is at greater risk of becoming one.

Drug abuse can weaken us physically. Worse, it can cause permanent mental damage. Our brain is the most important part of our body. Our thoughts, hopes, wishes, feelings, and memories are located there, within 100 billion nerve cells. Alcohol and drugs that are abused will harm—and even destroy—these cells. During the teen years, your brain continues to develop and grow, but drugs and alcohol can impair this growth.

I treat all types of teenagers at my hospital programs and in my office. Many suffer from depression or anxiety. A lot of them abuse drugs and alcohol, and this makes their depression or fears worse. I have celebrated birthdays and high school graduations with many of my patients. But I have also been to sad funerals for others who have died from problems with drug abuse.

Doctors understand more about drugs today than ever before. We've learned that some substances (even some foods) that we once thought were harmless can actually cause health problems. And for some people, medicines that help relieve one symptom might cause problems in other ways. This is because each person's body chemistry and immune system are different.

For all of these reasons, drug awareness is important for everyone. We need to learn which drugs to avoid or question—not only the destructive, illegal drugs we hear so much about in the news, but also ordinary medicines we buy at the supermarket or pharmacy. We need to understand that even "good" drugs can hurt us if they are not used correctly. We also need accurate scientific knowledge, not just rumors we hear from other teens.

Drug awareness enables you to make good decisions. It allows you to become powerful and strong and have a meaningful life!

Do you smoke? Do you think you can quit after trying "just a few" cigarettes? You may be dead wrong. Read this chapter to find out why nicotine, along with marijuana and alcohol, is called a "gateway" drug.

THE YES GENERATION: ARE DRUGS "IN"?

n a suburb of Boston, Massachusetts, in March 1997, 14 teenagers were rushed to the hospital after they overdosed on prescription muscle relaxants while attending a school dance. Ten of the students ended up in critical condition. "Someone said, 'Hey, let's do this,'" one of the teens admitted afterward. "We didn't ask what the pills were, we just started taking them and taking them and taking them."

• • •

A 14-year-old girl we'll call "Melody" was enrolled in a gifted student program. She was also learning karate and was a member of a marching band and a choir. Then one night Melody got drunk at a party. For the next three years, she abused alcohol, **marijuana**, and **cocaine**. She ended up in three different rehabilitation programs and in court. Then Melody found out that she was pregnant by a boy whose name she didn't even know, a boy who had forced her to have sex at a party when she was too high to resist.

In 1992, rock star Billy Idol collapsed outside a Hollywood club. He went into convulsions and almost died. He had been indulging in a dangerous synthetic (artificial) **steroid** called GHB, nicknamed "grievous bodily harm."

On March 13, 1997, two boys were arrested in a Maryland suburb and charged with planning to sell **crack**. The police officers apprehended the pair at an elementary school—they were in the fourth grade and were only 10 years old. "It's a surprise," remarked one of the policemen, "but that's the way things are going these days."

Just Say Yes?

The current slogan of choice for too many young people these days seems to be "just say yes." From Hollywood to your hometown, drugs appear to be back in style. And they are making a killing.

An ongoing survey called "Monitoring the Future" samples the drug-using habits and attitudes of American students. Here are some statistics from the 1996 survey:

- By the end of eighth grade, more than one-third of students (38 percent) have tried an illegal drug or **inhalants**.

- One in every 33 high school seniors has tried crack cocaine.
- About one in 22 high school seniors smoke marijuana daily.
- About 30 percent of high school seniors had consumed five or more drinks in a row at least once during the two weeks before the survey.
- One-third (34%) of seniors are cigarette smokers, with 22 percent smoking daily.

"So kids are experimenting with drugs. So what?" you might say. "That doesn't mean all of these kids have a *problem* with drugs or have an **addiction**, right?" Well, studies indicate that at least four million teenagers in this country are currently physically dependent or addicted to drugs. And one study shows that about one of every 10 kids who experiment with any type of drug will probably become addicted.

In many cases it takes only 6 to 18 months of heavy drug use for a teenager to become an addict. Just imagine: you and a bunch of your friends share a bottle of your parents' vodka in the woods behind your house one dull Saturday night in September. By Christmas time, one of you drinks cheap wine every morning before school, and by June the next year smokes **blunts** (marijuana-filled cigars) and hangs out with an older group of kids who use a lot of drugs. "Not me," you say, "that will *never* be me. I may *try* alcohol or pot, but I'll never become an alcoholic or drug addict."

Maybe you're right. But if you *try* drugs, the chances

This photo shows some illegal drugs and the paraphernalia (equipment) used to administer others. You may believe that you can try drugs without being harmed, but the risk of becoming addicted or psychologically dependent is greater than you think.

of your becoming addicted are much greater than if you never started in the first place. Read the following information, collected by the National Center on Addiction and Substance Abuse at Columbia University. Then ask yourself: am I willing to take that risk?

- A 12- to 17-year-old who smokes cigarettes is 19 times more likely to use cocaine than one who does not smoke.
- An adolescent who drinks alcohol is 50 times more likely to use cocaine than one who does not drink.
- A 12- to 17-year-old who smokes pot is 85 times more likely to use cocaine than one who does not use pot.

- Adolescents who drink and smoke pot and cigarettes are 266 times more likely to use cocaine than those who don't use any of these drugs.

What Is Addiction?

Addiction to alcohol and other drugs is a **progressive** disease, which means that if it is left untreated, it will get worse. The disease of addiction is also **chronic**, which means it is permanent. Once you become an addict, you will always be an addict. This disease is treatable—the addict can learn to control it. But addiction can also be fatal. Continued abuse of alcohol or other drugs may lead to premature death from an overdose, infection with a deadly disease such as **AIDS**, or suicide.

The United States has the highest rate of addiction in the world. The drug addiction club is a big one—it has many "members" and is very easy to join. But those who do join discover that it is extremely difficult to quit.

Mind and Body Dependence

Substances that alter your mood, your behavior, or your state of mind are called **psychoactive** drugs. Many of these drugs, including alcohol and tobacco, can cause **psychological dependence**. This means that users feel the need to take the drug for the rush or feeling of relaxation it creates. People who are psychologically dependent believe that they have to use the drug to feel "normal." They only feel right when they're high on the drug.

Using these substances can also lead to **physical**

Studies show that drug use almost always begins when people are younger than 20 years old. This book will help you find ways to avoid drinking alcohol or using other drugs that can harm you.

dependence, which is also called addiction. Addicts feel that they *must* continue to use the drug, despite the negative consequences of doing so. People who are addicted will suffer **withdrawal** symptoms if they stop using the drug. Withdrawal from alcohol or other drugs—including nicotine, the active ingredient in all tobacco products—can be uncomfortable, painful, or even life-threatening, depending on the individual and the drug of addiction. Itching, chills, nausea, sweating, stomach pain, anxiety, preoccupation, and depression are some of the minor symptoms. Withdrawal from more dangerous substances such as **heroin** or cocaine may include convulsions, **hallucinations** (visions that are not real), coma, or death.

The development of a physical dependence may take weeks, months, or even years. But with certain highly addictive drugs like crack, addiction can occur after just one use. And in certain individuals who are **predisposed** to physical dependence, an evening of partying and experimenting with drugs can escalate into addiction almost overnight.

Unfortunately, since there are few obvious signs of dependence early on, teens tend to believe that their drug use is controllable. But no one can know when dependence begins. It's almost as though the user crosses an invisible line, from wanting to smoke, drink, or do other drugs to *needing* to do so.

How do you think a drug or alcohol addiction typically begins? Choose what you believe is the best answer from the choices below:

- You attend a junior high party and down a few beers with your friends, although you hate the taste of beer.
- You take a hit of pot offered by an older friend, but you do not get high or feel any different.
- You develop a new crew of friends and begin to do what they do, even when they're drinking or taking other drugs.

Which answer did you choose? Surprise: all of them are correct.

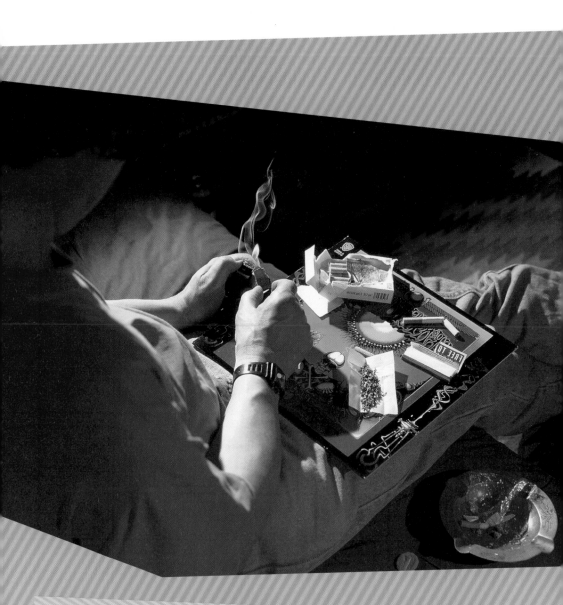

Marijuana is a gateway drug, which means that using it can lead to using drugs that are more dangerous. Sixty percent of kids who smoke pot before age 15 move on to cocaine. Kids aged 12 to 17 who smoke pot are 85 times more likely to use cocaine than those who do not smoke pot.

WHAT HAPPENS
IF YOU SAY YES

"I really thought I had to keep doing everything everyone else was doing," reports "Dean" in the drug information handbook *Drugs and Kids*. "Before I got a chance to wake up, I was picked up [by the police] and my sentences totaled 17 years. It got worse. I moved to heroin."

"I began drinking at home at age 14," explains "Gary" in *It Won't Happen to Me: True Stories of Teen Alcohol and Drug Abuse*. "That summer we spent seven weeks at the beach and I fell in with a crowd that was drinking and smoking marijuana. By the time I returned home [and started] tenth grade, I was drinking—and I don't mean having two or three beers. I was getting drunk two or three times a week and getting high on marijuana every day. . . . Before I finished, I had been on everything except roller skates."

Gateway Drugs

Addiction usually begins rather innocently with one or more of the substances called **gateway drugs**: tobacco, alcohol, and marijuana. These are typically the first drugs kids experiment with, and they often open the "gateway" to abusing other drugs. Despite the popular myth that cigarettes, alcohol, and pot are harmless, these drugs can be dangerous and addictive themselves. And if you never try gateway drugs, it is highly unlikely that you will ever abuse drugs of any kind.

Alcohol kills more people than all other drugs combined, except **nicotine** (found in cigarettes and chewing tobacco, which cause lung disease and cancer). Alcohol also kills more *kids* than all other drugs combined. Because alcoholic beverages are readily available and widely accepted as part of America's social lifestyle, they are usually the first drugs teens try. And make no mistake: *alcohol is a drug*. It alters your mind, mood, physical functions, and overall health.

For children and teenagers, whose bodies and minds are still developing, the physical effects of excessive alcohol intake are especially serious. Alcohol damages the body's essential internal organs, including the liver and the brain. And drinking "just a beer" or "just a wine cooler" is no less harmful: a 12-ounce can of beer, a 4 1/2-ounce glass of wine, and one ounce of hard liquor all contain the same amount of alcohol. So despite what you may hear, drinking "a couple of beers" is *still* drinking.

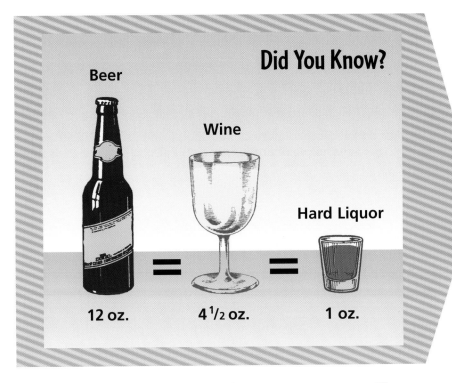

Did You Know?

Beer — 12 oz. = Wine — 4 1/2 oz. = Hard Liquor — 1 oz.

People who drink when they are teens are more likely to become alcoholics than those who wait until they are older before trying alcoholic beverages. Alcohol-addicted teens have a much tougher time kicking the habit than older users, and the disease progresses much more rapidly. Adolescents can "hit bottom" (reach the worst phase of the disease) only six months after they begin drinking. Studies indicate that almost 3.5 million teenagers are alcoholics. Many became alcoholics even before they were old enough to drive a car.

The addiction rate for preteen drinkers is even higher than for older drinkers. Until the 1980s, relatively few preteens used alcohol on a regular basis. During the past two decades, however, increasingly younger kids are experimenting with alcohol.

"I never really liked the taste of beer, but I drank it anyway because I liked the way it made me feel," reported "Melissa," a young addict who tells her story in the book *It Won't Happen to Me*. "In sixth grade my tops was six beers. One six-pack made me pretty drunk." By the time she graduated from high school, Melissa "used speed and coke [both **stimulants**], drank, and worked in a fast-food joint when I managed to get there. . . . When my brain wasn't getting fried from speed, I would smoke instead. I always had something." Eventually Melissa entered a psychiatric program and completely stopped using drugs.

In 1991, 10.5 million children in seventh through twelfth grade drank more than one billion cans of beer. Kids in this age group, 12 to 18, consume 35 percent of all the wine coolers sold in the United States—even though it is illegal for kids younger than 21 to buy or drink alcoholic beverages. By their senior year, 35 percent have had **binge** drinking episodes (drinking excessive amounts at one time) in the past month. Does someone *you* know drink too much? Have you ever seen this person drunk? How did that person look—cool or dumb?

"Somebody once told me that if you start smoking cigarettes, you're going to start doing everything else, too. It was true for me anyway," explained Melissa. "I had my first cigarette when I was nine." More than 400,000 Americans die prematurely every year from diseases caused by cigarette smoking. This is greater than the number of deaths from AIDS, alcohol, car accidents, murders, suicides, fires, and other drugs combined! Yet young smokers often believe that only a *lifetime* of tobacco use is dangerous. Studies show, however, that an addiction to nicotine is stronger in those who begin smoking at a younger age. So the chances are good that if you are smoking cigarettes at age 12, you will probably still be smoking when you are 17, 27, or even 77—if you live that long.

Among teenagers, the cigarette and tobacco habit is second in popularity only to alcohol. Every day, more than 3,000 teens light up for the first time. Tobacco stimulates the nervous system in the same way that cocaine does, and it can be just as addictive. Chewing tobacco is just as bad for your health as smoking it, and it is equally repulsive as a habit. Picture one or two people you know who smoke cigarettes or chew tobacco: do they look cool or silly with those things in their mouths or spitting tobacco juice into an empty beer can?

A third gateway drug is marijuana, also called "dope," "pot," "grass," "weed," "herb," and "reefer." Marijuana is derived from the hemp plant (its scientific name is *Cannabis sativa*). Lots of people know how marijuana makes you feel, but did you know that the cannabis plant contains more than 400 chemicals? Several of them are psychoactive. The chemical with the strongest effect on the brain is **THC (delta-9 tetrahydrocannabinol)**, which is found in the resin of the plant.

When smoked or eaten in foods, pot creates a feeling of **euphoria**, or well-being, and a sense of heightened consciousness. These days, however, the marijuana available on the street is much stronger than it was 30

Inhaling the fumes from products such as paint, paint remover, and charcoal lighter fluid can give you a quick "rush"— but it can also kill you within seconds. Are you willing to take that risk?

years ago. In the 1960s and 1970s, when pot was as popular as peace signs and hippies, the level of THC in cannabis plants was usually between 0.25 and 1 percent. Marijuana harvested in the United States today has THC levels that frequently exceed 20 percent. This increased potency not only makes marijuana more intoxicating but also increases the mental and physical health risks to those who use it. And today's users are starting on the drug at an increasingly younger age. The most recent report from the Monitoring the Future study on drug use showed that the average age when kids first try marijuana is now 13 1/2.

The THC in marijuana interferes with coordination, balance, and sense of time. It also increases the body's blood-pressure level and heart rate. The popular myth that marijuana is safer than most other illegal drugs is not true: there are actually *more* **carcinogenic** chemicals in marijuana smoke than in cigarette smoke. Long-term use of pot can damage your immune system, which fights off diseases and illness, making your body more susceptible to certain health problems. Smoking pot also lowers hormone levels, which can interfere with normal sexual development. And THC remains in the body for days or even weeks after marijuana is actually smoked or eaten.

Regular use of pot also impairs your emotional and intellectual capabilities. "Pot heads" can develop what is called **amotivational syndrome**. This means that the user loses motivation, becomes apathetic (not caring about much), and is less physically active than when not using pot. Marijuana also impairs your short-term memory and ability to concentrate. One 16-year-old boy who used to smoke pot described its effects this way: "Marijuana makes you stupid."

Sniffing and Huffing

Inhalants—substances whose fumes are inhaled to produce intoxication—are another category of drugs that young kids begin experimenting with. This is because most of these substances are common household or commercial products that are readily available in homes, groceries, drugstores, and home improvement shops. The most common inhalants kids "sniff" (inhale by the nose) or "huff" (inhale by the mouth) are **solvents** such as glue, paint thinner, window cleaner, furniture polish, nail polish, gasoline, correction fluid, and felt-tip markers. Other products used as inhalants are aerosols like hair spray and spray paint, or gases, like Freon, found in refrigerants for car and home use. The fumes of inhalants are breathed directly into the lungs from the original container, from a plastic or paper bag, or from an inhalant-soaked rag.

The youngest teens are the biggest abusers of inhalants. The 1996 Monitoring the Future study reported that more than one in five eighth graders (22 percent) have used inhalants at some point in their lives. About six percent used them in the month before the survey was taken.

Abusing inhalants produces a quick feeling of intoxication and a brief "high." This sensation is followed by drowsiness, dizziness, and often confusion. Although they may seem less harmful than illegal drugs, these products—even when used properly—are **toxic** chemicals and are extremely dangerous. They can even be deadly. It is very difficult to control how much of these substances you are inhaling. Just one try can cause **sudden sniffing death**, a condition in which an abuser's heart becomes overstimulated and the person dies almost immediately.

On June 5, 1994, the body of 15-year-old Jennifer Jones was discovered outside her house in Palm Beach Gardens, Florida. She had passed out into the plastic bag she was using to huff Freon, the trademark name for the coolant gas used in the family's air conditioner. Jennifer had tried huffing for the first time only four days earlier. According to her mother, who now speaks to the public about the dangers of inhalants, parents, teachers, and other adults don't realize how often kids try inhalants. "If you ask a 15-year-old about huffing, he knows exactly what you're talking about," Mrs. Jones says. "If you mention it to his parents, they haven't got a clue."

Cocaine and Crack

Cocaine, or "coke," is a powerful stimulant that increases the heart rate and blood pressure and dilates (expands) the bronchi, or breathing tubes, of the lungs. Stimulants create a sense of energy, alertness, and well-being that is followed by a "crash." Other stimulants include caffeine and amphetamines, which are also called "speed" or "uppers."

Cocaine is often "snorted" into the nose, but is also swallowed or melted and injected into the veins. It is highly addictive and dangerous—and using it can be fatal. When taken on a regular basis, cocaine disrupts mental function, causes hallucinations, **paranoia** (exaggerated fears), and violent behavior. In addition, coke addicts often turn to criminal behavior like shoplifting or robbery to pay for greater and greater amounts of the drug.

Crack is the most highly addictive drug available in the United States. Also known as "rock," crack is derived from cocaine powder that is mixed with sodium bicarbonate and hardened into small chunks. These chunks are heated in a pipe to form a vapor that is inhaled into the lungs. Smoking crack, or "freebasing," produces an extremely rapid and very intense rush. Users can and do become addicted after smoking it just once. Because of the way it reaches the brain (through the lungs), crack is believed to be 5 to 10 times more addictive than regular cocaine. Crack users also develop more physical and mental problems than those who use regular cocaine, including increasingly violent behavior and suicidal tendencies.

As with any addictive drug, cocaine and crack can ruin users' lives. They may develop bizarre, compulsive behaviors. They often stop taking care of themselves physically. Frequent snorting also causes nosebleeds and nasal damage. Injecting cocaine or any illegal drug makes the user more susceptible to diseases such as AIDS, which are transmitted through bodily fluids like blood.

Heroin: the New "In" Drug

A super-strong depressant drug, heroin is a white or brownish powder or black "tar" that is injected into the bloodstream, sniffed, or smoked. Derived from the opium poppy plant, "junk" or "smack" produces a three- to six-hour euphoric state, but users often look like they are asleep (a condition called "nodding out"). Heroin is highly addictive and can be deadly. Even more dangerous is a heroin and cocaine combination known as a "speedball."

In past years, heroin sold illegally in the United States was usually heavily diluted, or "cut," by drug dealers who wanted to make more money and have their drug supply last longer. Beginning in the 1990s, however, heroin became more widely produced. As a result, more of the

Whatever else you hear about marijuana and other drugs, remember this: they're illegal. Depending on where you are caught, you can face heavy fines and be jailed for using, buying, or selling them.

drug became available, and the purity rose sharply, to 50 or 60 percent. This very strong heroin is often smoked or inhaled like cocaine, rather than injected. Injecting heroin into the veins, or "mainlining," is especially dangerous because when hypodermic needles are shared, the risk of contracting AIDS becomes extremely high.

Unfortunately, many young people mistakenly believe that smoking or snorting is safer and less addictive than injecting. They're wrong on both counts. According to recent surveys from the early 1990s to the mid-1990s, the number of eighth and tenth graders using heroin doubled. And most users who start off snorting or smoking the drug end up injecting it once they become addicted.

Chronic use of heroin causes serious physical and mental problems, including frequent infections, severe depression and suicidal thoughts, inflammation of the lungs, liver, kidneys, or brain, and diseases such as AIDS or tetanus. Overdosing is common and quite easy to do.

Emerging Drugs

The Office of National Drug Control Policy (ONDCP) in Washington, D.C., publishes regular reports on the use and distribution of illegal drugs in the United States. A report released in 1997 cited the following drugs as "emerging," or becoming popular in cities across the country:

- Methamphetamine—a smokeable stimulant also known as "crank" or "ice." Use of this dangerous drug, which can also be snorted or injected, has been increasing by an estimated one percent each year in high schools throughout the country. Side effects include confusion, paranoia, aggressive and violent behavior, heart failure, and brain damage.

- "Club drugs"—a variety of drugs used at nightclubs and "raves" (large parties open to the public and held in locations like warehouses, basements, and unused buildings). Raves are frequently attended by underage kids. Most popular of late are hallucinogens (see below). And the ONDCP reports that kids are also inventing their own dangerous drug combinations, such as "red rock opium" (cough syrup, caffeine, sugar, tobacco, and stay-awake pills). Others are "beaning," which means that they chew coffee beans to feel the stimulant effect of caffeine.

- Hallucinogens—**LSD** (lysergic acid diethylamide) is a powerful mood-altering chemical sold in tablets, capsules, or liquid, which is sometimes soaked into small squares of blotter paper. "Acid," as it is called, causes hallucinations and creates an altered state of time and self. The drug's effects are unpredictable; a "bad trip" can cause intense panic and terror. Another hallucinogen is **MDMA** (3,4-methylene-dioxymethamphetamine), best known as Ecstasy. MDMA is one of a group of substances called "designer drugs." The chemical structures of designer drugs closely resemble those of prescription or illegal drugs like heroin or cocaine, but they are usually produced by amateur chemists in makeshift laboratories, so their purity and side effects are unknown or unpredictable. MDMA can be dangerous or fatal. Other popular hallucinogens include Ketamine (also called "Special K"), a drug that gives the user the sensation of superhuman strength; and hallucinogenic mushrooms, plants that are ingested to cause mind-altering effects in the user.

- "Date rape" drugs—illegally used prescription drugs that are often given to others without their consent to

This drawing won first place in an Orange County, California, drug awareness poster competition. Are you involved in any drug awareness activities in your area? Check with your school or local library to find out where you can help.

make them pass out. The most well-known of these drugs is Rohypnol, a sleeping pill (also known as a "roofie") that was used in a number of known rape incidents in Texas and Florida.

According to Dr. David Smith, founder of the Haight-Ashbury Free Clinics in San Francisco, California, "Kids today are using themselves as experimental laboratories for strange drug combinations that no scientist ever thought of." At all-night raves, kids are taking acid with Ecstasy, a powerful and dangerous mixture called a "candy flip." They're beaning; they're mixing prescription drugs with caffeine; they're "tripping" on LSD. At home and at school, kids are sniffing correction fluid or huffing Freon. Some kids are also smoking blunts that are dipped in cough syrup. Some are even smoking pot in their classrooms at school. Even elementary school children are being busted for selling drugs. Kids are drinking alcohol and using other drugs beginning at age nine or even younger.

What's going on in *your* neighborhood and at *your* school? How would you answer the following questions?

- Is your school drug-free?
- Do you know someone who sells illegal drugs?
- Do you know anyone who has used inhalants?
- Do you have a friend who has used acid, cocaine, heroin, or other "hard" drugs?
- How many of your friends use marijuana?
- Do most of your friends drink alcohol in social situations?
- Do some of your friends smoke cigarettes daily?
- Have you ever had a serious discussion with your parents about drinking and drug use?

When some of these questions were asked in a nationwide survey conducted in 1998, more than half of the 17-year-olds who responded said that they knew someone who had used hard drugs. On average, students said that half of their friends were smoking pot at least once a month. Only a small percentage believed that their schools were drug-free.

You may think the "Budweiser frogs" commercials are amusing, but a number of anti-drug groups, including Mothers Against Drunk Driving (MADD), do not. They believe that advertisements with kid-friendly characters—such as these frogs or the "Joe Camel" figure in some cigarette ads—target kids who are too young to use these drugs legally. What do you think? Do these kinds of ads make using drugs look fun?

THE CULTURE OF SAYING YES

In December 1997, both Robert Downey Jr. and Christian Slater, two well-known young Hollywood actors, were sent to prison on heroin and cocaine charges. Chris Farley, the mega-sized comedian from *Saturday Night Live*, had even worse luck: he was found dead that same month.

Downey, the star of such popular movies as *Two Girls and a Guy*, *Natural Born Killers*, and *Less than Zero* (in which he played a cocaine addict), was ordered by a judge to enter a drug rehabilitation program, but he left it after only a few days. Twenty-eight-year-old Slater, who appeared in the movies *True Romance*, *Heathers*, and *Broken Arrow*, was arrested after an alcohol and drug binge during which he beat up his girlfriend and then bit a man who came to her defense. And Farley died after a four-day nonstop holiday party that included alcohol, cocaine, and heroin abuse.

Since 1992, at least five young musicians have died from heroin-related causes: Jonathan Melvoin of the Smashing Pumpkins, Bradley Nowell of Sublime, Dwayne Goettel of Skinny Puppy, Kristen Pfaff of Hole, and Stefanie Sargent of 7 Year Bitch. Shannon Hoon of Blind Melon died of a cocaine overdose in 1995 after being treated for a heroin habit. The lead singer for Pantera once overdosed on heroin and claims he was dead for five minutes before being revived.

And, of course, there's Kurt Cobain of Nirvana, who committed suicide in 1994 after spending only 36 hours in a California drug recovery program (where his roommate was the lead singer of the Butthole Surfers). In the lyrics of his last album, Cobain, who had been addicted to heroin for years, asked his many fans, "What is wrong with me?"

The Glamorous Allure of Drugs

American pop culture seems to glorify the use of drugs. Some movies depict the "excitement" of drug abuse. Fashion designers use ultra-thin models with dark circles under their eyes to imitate the physical appearance of chronic heroin users. When model Zoe Fleischaur moved to New York at age 21, she quickly developed a heroin habit. "They wanted models that looked like junkies," she explained. "There are a lot of junkies in the industry. It's very hush-hush."

In the late 1960s and early 1970s, LSD was the "in"

A scene from the 1996 British movie *Trainspotting*. Movies, music, magazines, and advertisements often imply that using alcohol or other drugs will make you happier, more popular, or more attractive. In reality, none of this is true.

drug among hippies and philosophers because of its supposed ability to "raise consciousness," or allow greater insight into problems. It became fashionable among some groups to "turn on, tune in, drop out," as one slogan advised. In the 1980s, the cultural trend was one of getting ahead and earning lots of money as fast as possible. During this period, cocaine became a popular drug because it was associated with (and enhanced) quick thinking, and it seemed to provide users with endless energy to work and attend all-night parties.

In the 1990s, heroin has become the "in" drug. Some

Many kids believe that marijuana is a relatively harmless drug. In fact, the cannabis plant is an unpredictable drug factory that increases your heart rate and blood pressure, impairs your ability to learn and remember, affects your coordination, and may cause cancer.

current alternative rock music celebrates the "strung-out" sensation of heroin. "It's follow the leaders even in death," one movie producer told *Entertainment Weekly* magazine about the current trend in drug abuse that has claimed the lives of such stars as Kurt Cobain.

Is Everybody Doing It?

"Nell," a bright girl who attends public high school in a typical Midwestern city, uses drugs regularly. "Around here there is not [a thing] to do," she complained to *Sev-*

enteen magazine in May 1997. In the same interview, a fellow student of Nell's declared that drugs are "just part of everyday life." A boy called "Bob" in the article agreed. "Everybody's got a little bit of stress in their lives," Bob said. "Homework, girls, mean teachers—[drug use] is your ticket out of there for a little while."

There are lots of excuses for using drugs, and the kids who do so will claim that their reasons are good. All the hip musicians and cool actors do drugs, they'll say. Or most of their friends smoke pot, or their parents have cocktails every night. They may argue that they need something to help them relax, too. As Steve Logan, a 16-year-old from Oklahoma, told *Reader's Digest*, "All I know is that almost every song you listen to says something about [drugs]. It puts it into your mind constantly." Phil Cannon, another 16-year-old from Oklahoma, explained, "When you see the celebrities doing [drugs], it makes it seem okay."

The Remote Control Culture

We live in a society that demands instant satisfaction. Just think about how easy it is to order a pepperoni pizza by telephone, change a TV channel by remote control, or relieve a headache by popping an aspirin. The speedy high of most drugs fits in perfectly with this quick-fix attitude toward life.

Advertisements on radio, television, billboards, and in magazines and newspapers promote the idea that specific products like deodorants, toothpaste, cigarettes, beer, sports cars, or stylish clothes will make us happier, more popular, more attractive, or more successful. Over-the-counter medications like diet pills, vitamins, and pain relievers are trumpeted as easy solutions for losing weight, improving health, boosting energy, or easing aches and pains. Advertisers aim to convince us that we can make our lives better simply by buying their product. But is it really that easy?

Even Mom and Dad Do It

In 1996, the National Center on Addiction and Substance Abuse at Columbia University in New York conducted a survey of teens and their parents. The center found that almost half of the parents who were interviewed had tried marijuana when they were young. Of these parents who had smoked marijuana, more than half of them admitted that they would consider it a crisis to find out that their 15-year-old was using marijuana. The overwhelming majority of parents—94 percent—claimed that they had talked to their teenagers about the dangers of drugs, but only 61 percent of their teens said that they'd had such discussions with their parents.

Many parents who were teenagers during the 1960s and 1970s have tried drugs. Although most of them no longer use drugs, they feel hypocritical—that is, fake or phony—telling their children not to do something they once did themselves. As a result, they don't say anything at all to their kids about the subject. Others who admit to their kids that they once used drugs, but don't explain that drug use can be dangerous, may lead their children to believe that it's okay to take drugs. Some kids even have one or both parents who still smoke pot or use other illegal drugs, or parents who drink heavily. They are serving as role models for saying yes to drugs and encouraging kids by their own example to indulge in alcohol or other drugs.

Some of today's attitudes may not be all that different from when your parents were your age. However, the differences in attitude that do exist are serious. Kids are beginning to experiment with alcohol and other drugs at earlier ages. And the drugs they are trying are much more dangerous than when your parents were your age. Your parents might have "played with fire" by using drugs when they were teenagers. But if you are using drugs today, you're playing with fire *and* kerosene in flammable clothes!

Once You Get Started . . .

Most people do not enjoy their first drug experience. They may throw up, pass out, feel panicky, or feel ill for hours or even days afterward. Once you are using drugs regularly, the excitement and enjoyment you may have felt at one time turns into desperation and despair. You begin to feel as though you *need* drugs just to get through your life. And even then, when life is getting worse and worse, you continue to have strong physical and mental cravings to use the drug.

There is only one real reason why so many people continue using drugs once they've started: it is very difficult to say no once you've said yes. "[In my] freshman year I went downhill so fast that I never finished the

Oscar-nominated actor Robert Downey Jr. sits handcuffed in a California court-room in July 1996 after being arrested on drug and weapons charges. The following year, he went to prison on heroin and cocaine charges. Downey is one of many celebrities who have struggled with drug addiction.

term," admits "Kimberly," a 16-year-old addict. "I had lost my self-respect and my morals. I had no responsibil-ities: I stopped going to school or helping out at home. I didn't feel guilty because I had no feelings other than I want this drug; I need it now. I had no control over myself. Alcohol and drugs controlled me. I felt cold. I had no feelings for anyone. I didn't know a person could feel that way."

Are any of your friends or family members at risk of losing control to alcohol or other drugs? If a friend or relative shows one or more of these behaviors, he or she may have a drug problem:

- Getting high on drugs or getting drunk on a regular basis
- Lying about the amount of alcohol or other drugs being used
- Avoiding you or other friends in order to get high or drunk
- Giving up activities such as sports, homework, or hanging out with friends who don't drink or use other drugs
- Having to use increasing amounts of a drug to get the same effect
- Constantly talking about drinking alcohol or using other drugs
- Pressuring other people to drink alcohol or use other drugs
- Believing that it's necessary to drink or use other drugs to have fun
- Getting into trouble with the law or getting suspended from school for an alcohol- or other drug-related incident
- Taking risks, including sexual risks and driving under the influence of alcohol or other drugs
- Feeling tired, run-down, hopeless, depressed, or even suicidal
- Missing work or school, or performing tasks poorly because of drinking or other drug use

And what about you? Might *you* have a problem with saying no?

One way you can avoid using alcohol or other drugs is by getting involved in a sport or an exercise program. Read this chapter to find out why being physically fit can help you stay drug-free.

WAYS TO SAY NO

O n June 17, 1986, the happiest young athlete in America was probably Len Bias, the University of Maryland's All-American basketball star. He had been drafted by his dream team, the Boston Celtics, and the team's star player, Larry Bird, had promised to show up at rookie camp.

About 40 hours later, the 22-year-old was dead from heart and respiratory failure caused by cocaine. "He had a reputation for not being a drug user," said his high school coach. "But I [had] talked to him about guilt by association. Lenny did associate with some people like that [drug users]. He always said, 'People know I'm not using, so what's the problem?' I guess the main lesson is that it only takes once. When it comes time for right or wrong, there's no time-out. It's not a basketball game."

Unlike Bias, Mark, a natural athlete and avid hiker, was lucky. He started drinking beer shortly after he turned 15. By the time he was 17, Mark was drinking alcohol and smoking pot "pretty much around the clock." Finally, he got help for his drug problems. Mark attributes his success to his love of athletics. "Being a sports nut has been a saving grace," he says. "[It] keeps me on track for months."

Say No with Your Body

One way to look better, feel better, and be in better physical shape is to practice a sport or begin an exercise program. Regular exercise is the best way to lose or maintain weight. It also builds muscle, trims body fat, and regulates appetite so that you eat the right amount of food for your body's needs. Exercise can also help blow off tension and release anger. Some fitness enthusiasts even achieve a "natural high" from working out regularly.

"But exercise is boring," you may say, "and it hurts." If you believe this, maybe you haven't tried enough activities to find one sport you really enjoy. Have you checked out water ballet, tap dancing, running, biking, backpacking, cross-country skiing, aerobics, ultimate Frisbee, or rock climbing? Give yourself a chance to discover that moving your body is a lot more fun than sitting around. And the results are great: you feel good, and you look good.

Saying yes to exercise can make it easier to say no to drugs. If your body looks great and feels strong and healthy, why wreck it? Remember Len Bias—he said yes to drugs just once, and that was all it took to wreck *everything*.

Does this kid's meal look familiar to you? Eating too much "junk food" can make you feel out of shape, tired, or moody, and can cause health problems when you are older.

Eat Well

If you're like most kids, you only think about food when you are hungry or bored, and then you just fill yourself up on whatever is available or tasty. But there is more to eating than grabbing a bag of potato chips or chowing down on a double cheeseburger. What you eat today affects how you look and feel not only right now but also in the years to come. If you eat poorly, you can easily grow into illness-prone, unhealthy-looking adult.

In 1996, the U.S. Department of Health and Human Services and the Department of Agriculture released a set of dietary guidelines that Americans should follow if

You don't need to drink alcohol or use other drugs to feel good about yourself. Sometimes all it takes is a little "puppy love."

they want to stay healthy and reduce their risk of developing certain ailments and diseases. Here is a list of what you should try to eat every day:

- Bread, cereal, rice, and pasta (carbohydrates): 6 to 11 servings
- Fruits (fresh, frozen, canned, dried, or juices): 2 to 4 servings
- Vegetables: 3 to 5 servings
- Meat, poultry, fish, beans, eggs, and nuts (proteins): 2 to 3 servings
- Milk, yogurt, and cheese (dairy products): 2 to 3 servings

- Fats, oils, and sweets: use sparingly

Becoming health-conscious can help you respect your body and avoid the things that harm it, such as alcohol, cigarettes, other drugs, and junk food. If you are exercising and eating healthfully, it seems a lot easier to say no to drugs.

Even if you are a health enthusiast or athlete, you might find excuses to drink alcohol or use other drugs. This is why saying no to drugs with your brain and your heart are also important to your health.

Say No with Your Brain

Seventeen-year-old Ned Vizzini is a junior at Stuyvesant High School in New York City. In the May 17, 1998, issue of the *New York Times Magazine*, he offered the following advice to 13-year-olds who are just beginning to deal with the problems of being an American teenager:

> In the next four years, you'll inevitably meet up with cigarettes and marijuana. You already know what smoking's like. Haven't you ever been stuck with a puffing relative at a family funeral? Smoking a cigarette yourself is similar—it tastes nasty and burns your throat. As for pot, it shares smoking's characteristics with one extra benefit: it makes you act really dumb.
>
> But you've been told that before. All teenagers have. Yet somehow they all end up at a party where somebody offers them a joint, and they have nothing to say but, "Uh, sure." Well, here's what you say:

"Nah, I tried that stuff once; it really messed me up." Proceed to tell a ridiculous anecdote about the time you "tried that stuff." If the story's funny enough to get everybody laughing, you'll slip out of the situation. Alternatively, simply shake your head, act uninterested and get into a conversation with somebody else. The quick, silent rebuttal is devastating.

Drinking is also a tricky issue. . . . But there's an easy way to handle parties without getting stinking drunk. Take a drink—anything, whatever they give you—and walk around pretending to sip it. (You'll need a plastic cup for this trick to work. A glass will give you away.) After an hour, discreetly put the drink down on a table. Nobody will notice this sleight of hand.

Saying no to drinking and using other drugs is a challenge. Abusing drugs causes people to care too little about themselves and others, and this can bring on even greater and more widespread problems. They include violent behavior, increased crime rates, suicides, juvenile delinquency, family problems such as physical abuse and divorce, prostitution, poverty, and homelessness. Studies show that a significant percentage of all of these social problems are directly linked to alcohol and other drug abuse.

You don't need to go along with (what looks like) everyone else in order to be a part of a certain group. Going along with the crowd is not very impressive anyway: it makes you just like everyone else. And though it may *seem* like "everybody" is doing drugs, they're not. If

What Makes You Feel Better About Yourself?

In May 1998, *USA Weekend Magazine* conducted a survey of more than 250,000 students in grades 6 to 12 to find out what they thought of themselves and what most influenced their self-image. The survey asked kids what they liked most and least about themselves. Half of the students said they felt "really good" about themselves, and half said they did not. The chart below shows the number of teens who chose ways they thought they could improve themselves and enhance their self-image:

Question: Which of the following would make you feel better about yourself?*

Getting better grades	49%
Bulking/toning up	38%
Losing weight	38%
Doing better at sports	36%
Better relationship with parents	30%
Wearing better clothes	24%
Fitting in with a certain crowd	16%
Nothing; I like myself the way I am	15%
Quitting smoking	8%

(*Teens responded to more than one choice in survey)

None of the students mentioned using drugs as a way to improve themselves. Using drugs will *not* help you to look better, feel better, or lead a more interesting life. But you can choose other ways to do so.

Source: *USA Weekend Magazine*, May 1, 1998

one out of every 10 high school graduates is using drugs, that means that 9 out of 10 are not.

Here are some additional tips on how to refuse alcohol or other drugs and mean it:

- Be aware. Knowing what drugs can do to you will make it easier to resist them.
- Be prepared. Find out in advance when and where you might end up in a situation where others are doing drugs. Then decide whether you really want to be there.
- Be decisive. Having a debate with someone about using drugs leaves the issue open. Make your "no, thanks" be the end of the discussion.
- Be busy. Have some places you have to be—for example, an after-school club or practice, a friend's house, a job, or your own home, where you have something creative to work on.
- Be smart. Anyone who pressures you to take drugs is not your friend, no matter how friendly they act. Don't be swayed by fake friendship.

After you say no a few times to beer, pot, or other drugs, you'll find it easier to turn down anything you don't want. And it is always easier to say no to something that you really are not interested in doing anyway.

Say No with Your Heart

"Drug abuse is not a problem with drugs, it's a problem with pleasure," says Roy Matthews, head of an alcoholism and addiction program at Duke University

These kids in Boston, Massachusetts, made paper cat masks to celebrate the anniversary of a local animal shelter. The "rush" you get from finishing a creative project can be far better than using drugs!

Medical Center in Durham, North Carolina. "Pleasure is the basis of addiction, and it would seem pleasure is a solution to addiction." Medical researchers have discovered how alcohol and drugs stimulate the release of certain chemicals in the brain that create a pleasurable high. Researchers have also discovered that there are ways other than taking dangerous drugs to turn on the pleasure chemicals in your brain.

You can probably think of some clean and sober activities that give you a euphoric "rush." Most of us have experienced certain situations that make us feel high: falling in love, working on a favorite project, listening to a beautiful piece of music, and praying are some of the more common ones.

When you are creating something, you totally tune in to your project and tune out the rest of the world. You put your heart and soul into your creation. Artists all over the world testify to the highs they get from drawing on their creative powers to make something that's all their own.

This wondrous feeling of being lost in your own world can also occur whenever you are doing something you enjoy deeply—for example, gardening, running, playing tennis, building a birdhouse, grooming your dog—whatever fires up your heart and spirit. When you're involved in your favorite activities, time seems to fly, and you are truly enjoying life.

Another way of tapping into your inner self is through meditation, an ancient practice that has long been used by people to create a feeling of stillness and a sense of deep relaxation within themselves. You probably think that only bearded men, sitting with their legs crossed in the "lotus" position, can learn this technique. But meditation is actually simple enough for anyone to learn.

Plenty of books are available that teach the simple steps of learning how to meditate. Many cities and towns also hold meditation classes. People who meditate regularly say that they feel a oneness with God, nature, or all creation—a feeling that alcohol and other drugs will totally destroy.

The Spiritual Way

Developing your spiritual side does not necessarily mean that you must practice a specific religion or attend a certain church or temple, although doing so can certainly help. Spirituality is about feeling a higher or deeper love for all of life. J. Earl Cavanaugh, dean of the Grace and Holy Trinity Cathedral in Kansas City, Missouri, explains why he believes it is important to be aware of your spiritual side. "We tend to look at everything in life as a problem to be solved," he says. "Yet when we talk about spirituality, we are talking about something that can't really be [measured]. We are talking about exploring life, not just in logical terms, but in terms of imagination and the soul."

You can find this sense of spirit not only in a house of worship, but also in other situations: volunteering at a hospital, working on a painting, gardening, walking in the woods, sailing, listening to music, or even attending a concert or party where you are laughing, dancing, and really enjoying your friends—and *not* drinking alcohol or using other drugs.

When Lois Kellerman, the head of the Brooklyn Society for Ethical Culture in New York, asked her young son what he thought about God, he responded, "I think God is what happens when we hug each other." What does spirituality or God mean to you? In what ways do you express your spiritual side?

Teenagers decorate their school gym for an anti-drug rally sponsored by D.A.R.E. (Drug Abuse Resistance Education). Check to see whether your school offers drug prevention programs like this one.

GETTING HELP

Chuck Negron, the former lead singer of Three Dog Night, considers himself lucky to be alive. "I had a twenty-year heroin habit," admits the rocker who sang "Celebrate" and "Jeremiah Was a Bullfrog" with one of the top bands of the early 1970s. "I missed what should have been the best part of my life." Although Three Dog Night produced 11 top ten hits between 1968 and 1975, by 1990 Negron was living on the floor of a crack house in East Los Angeles. "I had been through thirty-five hospitals over the years, but finally I entered a program called Cry Help. These people saved my life," Negron says. "After nine months there, my life changed forever." Negron now works as a drug counselor in programs designed to assist addicted musicians.

On his 16th birthday, Josh Allison sat on a bunk in the juvenile detention center in Paramus, New Jersey, thinking, "What's a kid [like me] doing in jail?" Picked up by police 20 times and locked up three times, Josh had been in trouble with the law ever since he began hanging out with a group of kids who did drugs. "They treated me like I belonged. And I wanted to be down with them," Josh later recalled. By the time he was 14, Josh was smoking pot every day and stealing the money he needed to buy it. When he tried cocaine, he got hooked. By the night of his 16th birthday, Josh realized that he was an addict. "And I had to be honest: I couldn't imagine being anywhere in ten years except in jail or dead," he says.

Fortunately, there was a third option. Josh asked his jail guards for help with his drug problem. He was transferred to the Phoenix House in Rockleigh, New Jersey, part of a national network of residential drug treatment facilities. At Phoenix House, he worked on getting his high school diploma—and staying sober—while attending group therapy sessions.

Your Body on Drugs

Drinking alcohol or using drugs can seem like a fun way to celebrate or kick back and relax, but the choice to use can prove deadly, even the very first time. It may also lead to dependence, abuse, and an addiction that is neither fun nor relaxing. Drinking and using other drugs can also ruin your looks as well as your health. Here is a portrait of an average teenage girl who parties regularly by drinking and smoking pot:

Two men living in the Harlem section of New York decorated the windows and fire escapes of their apartment building to draw attention to the dangers of crack cocaine. "Use your head," they painted on the wall of the building at street level, "or else you will be dead."

- Has red, bloodshot eyes
- Seems clumsy, trips over her own feet
- Acts "spaced out," forgets everything, acts stupid
- Has gained weight from "munching out"
- Has blotchy or broken-out skin
- Smells of sweet smoke (pot) or alcohol
- Looks sloppy, as though she hasn't showered lately

Here is another portrait, this time of an average teenage boy who is using "hard drugs":

- Has a runny nose; is always sniffling
- Sweats heavily, even in cold weather
- Has "the shakes"; can't seem to sit still
- Is thin or underweight; clothes seem to hang on him
- Looks exhausted, as though he hasn't slept in days
- Looks pale and sick

Do you think drug use is helping these two kids build their self-esteem and feel positive about themselves? Maybe partying with the in crowd is supposed to make you look cool, but drinking and using other drugs usually ends up backfiring, and you start to look—well, awful!

"This Is Your Brain On Drugs"

It can be extremely difficult to kick a drug habit. Your best bet for keeping your life on track is *never to start using*. And there are plenty of programs in schools, community centers, and even in the media (TV, radio, newspapers, magazines, and the Internet) that can help you learn how to avoid drugs.

The U.S. government has been waging what it calls a "war on drugs" for 50 years, often relying on advertisements to teach the public about the dangers of drug use. Since 1987, public schools have been required by the federal government to teach drug prevention. Some school- and community-based drug education programs are supported by government funds.

What drug education information are you aware of?

Have you seen the latest anti-drug TV ads, such as the one that features a young girl in the kitchen who destroys an egg, then the entire room to demonstrate the effects of heroin on your life and your family? This particular ad plays off the famous drug campaign series called "This is Your Brain on Drugs," which aired some years ago. In it, an egg said to be your brain is dropped into a sizzling frying pan to show what happens to your mind when you take drugs.

Check to see whether your school or community offers any drug prevention programs like these:

D. A. R. E.—the popular Drug Abuse Resistance Education program that sends police officers into schools to give you information about the dangers of drugs and about ways to resist peer pressure.

Life Skills Training—an effective program taught by teachers and peers that focuses on the immediate adverse effects of drugs by using discussion and "improvisation" (play-acting and role playing).

Media Literacy—a program sponsored by the U.S. Department of Health and Human Services that helps you distinguish between fact and fiction in the information you get from newspapers, magazines, TV, and radio.

Kick Drugs Out of America—a martial-arts training program for young people that was established by action film star and martial-arts champion Chuck Norris. The program teaches you discipline and self-confidence, which can help you avoid drug use.

Don't be afraid to seek help for a drug problem. Talking to a family member or other adult you trust shows that you are strong enough to help yourself.

What do you think about all of this information? Are anti-drug ads a good idea? Have you ever attended a drug education program? Did the information you received seem useful? Has any of this helped you avoid using—or wanting to use—drugs?

Drug Treatment Programs

Unfortunately, drug prevention programs don't work for all kids. Some will begin experimenting and before long, they end up with an addiction. But being addicted is not necessarily a death sentence. A wide variety of treatment programs are available to help people become and stay drug-free.

Recovering from alcohol or other drug addictions involves changing your behavior, attitude, and way of seeing yourself and your life. It means giving up not only drinking and using other drugs, but also the whole way of life that comes with it—and replacing it with a new way of living.

The best drug treatment program for each person depends on many factors, including the individual's personality, social situation, age, family situation, and degree and length of addiction. No treatment can guarantee a cure, but all of them offer hope to people who feel as though drugs have taken over their lives.

Most drug treatment programs fit into one of the following categories:

Self-help programs—free, drop-in meetings catered to specific addictions. Participants listen to others speak about their alcohol or other drug abuse. In this way, each person gives and receives support. Examples of self-help programs include Alcoholics Anonymous, Narcotics Anonymous, Cocaine Anonymous, and Drugs Anonymous.

Outpatient treatment—a structured plan of individual and group counseling that often includes family counseling as well. This kind of treatment is especially useful for young drug abusers at an early stage of addiction, or for those who are at low risk of relapsing (returning to drug abusing).

Day treatment—a day-long program of intense

counseling. This type of treatment is best for
former drug abusers who are not at great risk for
relapsing and are able to live at home rather than
in a treatment facility.

Inpatient treatment—a highly structured program in
which patients stay in a hospital-like facility and
are restricted from outside influences. They
participate in intensive counseling and treatment
over a period of weeks or months. A medical staff
is usually on hand in case patients experience
severe or life-threatening withdrawal symptoms.

Residential treatment—a supervised, round-the-clock
treatment program where patients live at the
center for up to a year. This kind of program is best
for people who are at great risk of relapsing. Most
patients in residential programs have tried other
types of treatment with little or no success.

Getting Help

Admitting that you need help with an alcohol or
other drug problem can be scary. And realizing that you
cannot solve your problem alone may feel overwhelming. But anyone who is abusing drugs requires experienced help. A good counselor, coach, teacher, or other
adult you feel comfortable talking to can direct you to a
support group or treatment program that is best for you.

Your parents (surprise, surprise) may be the most
important people you talk to about your problem. They
probably know you the best, love you the most, and will
do anything for you if you ask them for help. Of course,

Sometimes it's hard to resist pressure from your friends to drink alcohol or use other drugs. This poster offers a few suggestions on how to say no to drugs.

if your parents drink too much or use other drugs, they need to be aware that you are likely to copy them. They'll need to stay drug-free if they want you to do so. Parents can also be the strongest influence in keeping their kids off drugs. A recent study published in the *Journal of the American Medical Association* found that teens who feel close to their parents are more likely to stay away from drugs.

There are a number of ways you can feel closer to your parents. One is to talk to them about alcohol and other drugs. You could start by showing them this book.

After all, they want the best for you, and drugs and alcohol do not fit into that category.

It doesn't take a lot of brains to start using drugs, but drug addiction can destroy your mind or your life. Why not *use* your mind instead of losing it to drugs? Don't be afraid to ask for help if you need it. Everyone, kids and grown-ups, can use a little help now and then. Isn't that what friends and family are for? Your real friends—the people who truly love you—will help you say no to using drugs and yes to using your head.

Help Your Friends Say No

Maybe you don't drink or do other drugs—never have and never will. That's awesome, the best! But what about your friends or relatives? Does someone you know have a problem with alcohol or other drugs? Here are some steps you can take to help someone in trouble:

- Step 1: Talk to someone in private about your friend's or relative's drug use—a counselor, teacher, coach, doctor, parent, or religious leader. You don't even have to mention the person's name. But doing so will help you figure out what you can do to help.

- Step 2: Talk to your friend or relative about your concerns. But don't try to talk about the problem when the person is drunk or high.

- Step 3: Express your concern. Talk about how worried you are about the person's health, and how awful it is to see him or her drunk or high.

- Step 4: Give specific examples of how your friend

or relative behaves while intoxicated. Sometimes, hearing about one's antics from someone else removes the humor and shows the sad, pathetic, embarrassing aspects of being drunk or high.

- Step 5: Tell your friend or relative that you want to help. Suggest places to go for assistance. Offer to go along to a counseling or drug treatment center, and be sure to follow through on your offer if the person accepts.

- Step 6: Be prepared for the person to become angry or deny that he or she has a problem. Many people with alcohol or other drug problems react this way. But stick with it—the more people express concern, the better the chances of your friend or relative getting help.

Reaching out to your friend or loved one is an important gift. You cannot make someone accept your help, but sometimes just offering it is enough to let a person in trouble know you care.

Be sure to protect yourself, too. Never ride in a car or boat or on a motorcycle with someone who has been drinking or doing other drugs. And beware of anyone who tries to get you to use drugs yourself. You know what it means to *be* a real friend. You deserve to *have* real friends, too.

It's surprisingly easy to ruin your life by using drugs. But it can be just as easy not to. It's up to you. Don't blow it.

GLOSSARY

AIDS—acquired immunodeficiency syndrome, a defect of the immune system caused by the human immunodeficiency virus, or HIV. AIDS is spread by the exchange of blood and by sexual contact; intravenous drug users have an increased risk of contracting HIV and developing AIDS.

addiction—a condition of some drug users that is caused by repeated drug use. A drug user's body develops a tolerance to the drug and needs increasingly large amounts of the drug to achieve the same level of "high." When a person who is physically dependent on a drug stops taking the drug, withdrawal results.

amotivational syndrome—a loss of motivation that is accompanied by apathy, lack of concern for the future, and diminished physical activity. Some researchers believe that marijuana may cause amotivational syndrome.

binge—an uncontrolled or excessive indulgence in an activity, such as shopping, drinking, or eating.

blunt—a marijuana-filled cigar.

carcinogenic—causing or contributing to the growth of cancer.

chronic—occurring over a long period or frequently recurring.

cocaine—a powerful stimulant made from the leaves of the coca plant and usually sold as a white powder. Cocaine is highly addictive.

crack—a highly addictive, solid form of cocaine made by mixing the drug with other substances and then heating and hardening it. These small pieces, called "rocks," are smoked in a small pipe.

euphoria—an intense feeling of happiness or well-being.

gateway drug—a relatively weak drug whose use may lead to experimentation with stronger drugs like cocaine and heroin.

hallucination—a distorted perception of objects or events, or an object or vision that is not real but is perceived by a person who has a mental disorder or who is using drugs.

hallucinogen—a substance that distorts the user's perception of objects or events, or causes the user to perceive objects or visions that are not real.

heroin—the trade name given to diacetylmorphine, one of the strongest of the opiate drugs. Heroin is highly addictive.

inhalant—a common but toxic chemical that is inhaled through the nose or mouth to cause intoxication. Many common household products, such as correction fluid, felt-tip markers, model airplane glue, and nail polish remover, are abused as inhalants.

inpatient treatment—a drug rehabilitation program in which a person stays at, or is checked into, the clinic or hospital where the treatment will take place.

LSD—lysergic acid diethylamide, a hallucinogenic (mind-altering) drug made from a fungus that grows on the rye plant.

marijuana—a psychoactive drug derived from the hemp plant that is smoked or eaten for its initial effect of euphoria or relaxation.

MDMA—3, 4-methylenedioxymethamphetamine, also known as Ecstasy; a combination of a hallucinogen called MDA and the stimulant methamphetamine.

nicotine—an extremely addictive drug that occurs naturally in tobacco leaves. Nicotine has both stimulating and depressive effects on the body.

outpatient treatment—a drug rehabilitation program in which a person lives at home and attends scheduled therapy and education sessions.

paranoia—extreme, irrational distrust of others, accompanied by exaggerated fears.

physical dependence—a state in which a drug user's body chemistry has adapted to require regular doses of the drug to function normally. Stopping the drug causes withdrawal symptoms.

predisposed—having a tendency toward a particular action or thing. Some people are predisposed to develop drug addictions.

progressive—happening or advancing in a steady way or step by step.

psychoactive—affecting the mind or behavior.

psychological dependence—a state in which certain brain changes create strong cravings to use a drug, even if the user has no withdrawal symptoms or physical urge to do so.

solvent—a liquid, such as water, alcohol, or ether, that can dissolve another substance to form a solution. Common solvents include paint thinner, gasoline, and Freon (used in refrigeration units).

steroid—a powerful compound closely related to the male sex hormone testosterone. Anabolic steroids are sometimes used illegally by bodybuilders, long-distance runners, and other athletes to temporarily increase the size of their muscles.

stimulant—a drug that increases or speeds up the functions or activities of the body. Examples of stimulants are caffeine, cocaine, crack, amphetamines, and methamphetamine.

sudden sniffing death—a condition in which an inhalant abuser's heart becomes overstimulated by the inhalant and by the body's release of a chemical called norepinephrine, causing immediate death.

THC—an abbreviation for **delta-9 tetrahydrocannabinol**, the chemical found in cannabis that is most responsible for the high you get from marijuana.

toxic—poisonous.

withdrawal—a process that occurs when a person who is physically dependent on a drug stops taking the drug.

BIBLIOGRAPHY

Center for Substance Abuse Prevention (CSAP). "Tips for Teens About Alcohol." NCADI Publication #PHD323. Rockville, MD: CSAP, 1996.

Center for Substance Abuse Prevention. "Tips for Teens About Crack and Cocaine." NCADI Publication #PHD640. Rockville, MD: CSAP, 1996.

Center for Substance Abuse Prevention. "Tips for Teens About Hallucinogens." NCADI Publication #PHD642. Rockville, MD: CSAP, 1996.

Center for Substance Abuse Prevention. "Tips for Teens About Marijuana." NCADI Publication #PHD641. Rockville, MD: CSAP, 1996.

Gallagher, Jim. *Heroin*. Philadelphia: Chelsea House Publishers, 1999.

Hasday, Judy L., and Therese De Angelis. *Marijuana*. Philadelphia: Chelsea House Publishers, 1999.

Mothers Against Drunk Driving. "Some Myths About Alcohol." http://www.madd.org/UNDER21/youth_myths.shtml. Irving, TX: Mothers Against Drunk Driving, 1998.

National Institute on Drug Abuse (NIDA). "How Not to Get High, Get Stupid, Get AIDS: A Guide to Partying." NCADI Publication #PHD622. Bethesda, MD: NIDA, 1993.

Newman, Susan. *It Won't Happen to Me: True Stories of Teen Alcohol and Drug Abuse*. New York: Perigee, 1987.

Somdahl, Gary L. *Drugs and Kids: How Parents Can Keep Them Apart*. Salem, OR: Dimi Press, 1996.

FIND OUT MORE ABOUT
DRUG ABUSE AND HOW TO SAY NO

The following list includes agencies, organizations, and websites that provide information about specific drugs and drug abuse. You can also find out where to go for help with a drug problem.

Many national organizations have local chapters listed in your phone directory. Look under "Drug Abuse and Addiction" to find resources in your area.

Agencies and Organizations in the United States

Alateen
P.O. Box 862
Midtown Station
New York, NY 10018
212-302-7240
800-344-2666

Alcoholics Anonymous
P.O. Box 459
Grand Central Station
New York, NY 10163
212-870-3400

**American Council
   for Drug Education**
164 West 74th Street
New York, NY 10023
212-758-8060
800-488-DRUG (3784)
http://www.acde.org/
wlittlefield@phoenixhouse.org

**Center for Substance
   Abuse Treatment**
Information and Treatment Referral Hotline
11426-28 Rockville Pike, Suite 410
Rockville, MD 20852
800-622-HELP (4357)

**Children of Alcoholics
   Foundation, Inc.**
555 Madison Avenue, 4th floor
New York, NY 10022
212-754-0656 or 800-359-COAF (2623)

Drugs Anonymous
P.O. Box 473
Ansonia Station, NY 10023
212-874-0700

Families Anonymous
P.O. Box 3475
Culver City, CA 90231-3475
310-313-5800 or 800-736-9805

Girl Power!

U.S. Department of Health
   and Human Services
Office on Women's Health
11426 Rockville Pike, Suite 100
Rockville, MD 20852
800-729-6686
http://www.health.org/gpower
gpower@health.org

Marijuana Anonymous World Services

P.O. Box 2912
Van Nuys, CA 91404
800-766-6779
http://www.marijuana-anonymous.org/
MAWS98@aol.com

Narcotics Anonymous

P.O. Box 9999
Van Nuys, CA 91409
818-780-3951

National Adolescent Suicide Hotline

800-621-4000

National Center on Addiction and Substance Abuse at Columbia University

152 West 57th Street, 12th Floor
New York, NY 10019-3310
212-841-5200 or 212-956-8020
http://www.casacolumbia.org/home.htm

National Clearinghouse for Alcohol and Drug Information (NCADI)

Box 2345
Rockville, MD 20847-2345
800-729-6686
800-487-4889 TDD
800-HI-WALLY (449-2559, Children's Line)
http://www.health.org/

Office of National Drug Control Policy

750 17th Street, N.W., 8th Floor
Washington, DC 20503
http://www.whitehousedrugpolicy.gov/
ondcp@ncjrs.org
888-395-NDCP (6327)

Parents Resource Institute for Drug Education (PRIDE)

3610 Dekalb Technology Parkway, Ste. 105
Atlanta, GA 30340
770-458-9900
http://www.prideusa.org/

Shalom, Inc.

311 South Juniper Street
Room 900
Philadelphia, PA 19107
215-546-3470

Students Against Drunk Driving (SADD)

Box 800
Marlboro, MA 01750
508-481-3568

Agencies and Organizations in Canada

**Addiction Research
Foundation (ARF)**
33 Russell Street
Toronto, Ontario M5S 2S1
416-595-6100
800-463-6273 in Ontario

**Canadian Centre
on Substance Abuse**
75 Albert Street, Suite 300
Ottawa, Ontario K1P 5E7
613-235-4048
http://www.ccsa.ca/

Websites

**D.A.R.E. (Drug Abuse Resistance
Education) for Kids**
http://www.dare-america.com/index2.htm

**Join Together Online
(Substance Abuse)**
http://www.jointogether.org/sa/

**National Institute
on Drug Abuse (NIDA)**
http://www.nida.nih.gov

**Partnership for a
Drug-Free America**
http://www.drugfreeamerica.org/

Reality Check
http://www.health.org/reality/

**Safe & Drug-Free
Schools Program**
http://inet.ed.gov/offices/OESE/SDFS

**U.S. Department
of Justice Kids' Page**
http://www.usdoj.gov/kidspage/

Despite what you may have heard, selling illegal drugs will not make you rich. In 1998, two professors, Steven Levitt from the University of Chicago and Sudhir Venkatesh from Harvard University, released a study of how drug gangs make and distribute money. To get accurate information, Venkatesh actually lived with a drug gang in a midwestern city.

You may be surprised to find out that the average street dealer makes just about $3 an hour. You'd make more money working at McDonald's! Still think drug-dealing is a cool way to make money? What other after-school jobs carry the risk of going to prison or dying in the street from a gunshot wound?

Drug-dealing is illegal, and it kills people. If you're thinking of selling drugs or you know someone who is, ask yourself this question: is $3 an hour worth dying for or being imprisoned?

WHAT A DRUG GANG MAKES IN A MONTH*

	During a Gang War	No Gang War
INCOME (money coming in)	$ 44,500	$ 58,900
Other income (including dues and blackmail money)	10,000	18,000
TOTAL INCOME	**$ 54,500**	**$ 76,900**
EXPENSES (money paid out)		
Cost of drugs sold	$ 11,300	$ 12,800
Wages for officers and street pushers	25,600	37,600
Weapons	3,000	1,600
Tributes (fees) paid to central gang	5,800	5,900
Funeral and other expenses	10,300	4,200
TOTAL EXPENSES	**$ 56,000**	**$ 62,100**
TOTAL INCOME	$ 54,000	$ 76,900
MINUS TOTAL EXPENSES	- 56,000	- 62,100
TOTAL AMOUNT OF PROFIT IN ONE MONTH	**- 1,500**	**14,800**

* adapted from "Greedy Bosses," *Forbes*, August 24, 1998, p. 53. Source: Levitt and Venkatesh.

INDEX

PICTURE CREDITS

page

VIRGINIA ARONSON is the author of 16 published books, including nutrition and health texts and books for young people. A former health educator at Harvard University's School of Public Health, she lives in south Florida with her writer husband and their young son.

BARRY R. McCAFFREY is director of the Office of National Drug Control Policy (ONDCP) at the White House and a member of President Bill Clinton's cabinet. Before taking this job, General McCaffrey was an officer in the U.S. Army. He led the famous "left hook" maneuver of Operation Desert Storm that helped the United States win the Persian Gulf War.

STEVEN L. JAFFE, M.D., received his psychiatry training at Harvard University and the Massachusetts Mental Health Center and his child psychiatry training at Emory University. He has been editor of the *Newsletter of the American Academy of Child and Adolescent Psychiatry* and chairman of the Continuing Education Committee of the Georgia Psychiatric Physicians' Association. Dr. Jaffe is professor of child and adolescent psychiatry at Emory University. He is also clinical professor of psychiatry at Morehouse School of Medicine, and the director of Adolescent Substance Abuse Programs at Charter Peachford Hospital in Atlanta, Georgia.